Terms and Conditions

LEGAL NOTICE

The Publisher has strived to be as accurate and complete as possible in the creation of this report, notwithstanding the fact that he does not warrant or represent at any time that the contents within are accurate due to the rapidly changing nature of the Internet.

While all attempts have been made to verify information provided in this publication, the Publisher assumes no responsibility for errors, omissions, or contrary interpretation of the subject Matter herein. Any perceived slights of specific persons, peoples, or organizations are unintentional.

In practical advice books, like anything else in life, there are no guarantees of income made. Readers are cautioned to reply on their own judgment about their individual circumstances to act accordingly.

This book is not intended for use as a source of legal, business, accounting or financial advice. All readers are advised to seek services of competent professionals in legal, business, accounting and finance fields.

You are encouraged to print this book for easy reading.

Table Of Contents

Foreword

Chapter 1:
The Basics

Chapter 2:
Using News Letters

Chapter 3:
Visualize Goals

Chapter 4:
Blogs

Chapter 5:
How You See Your Success

Wrapping Up

Foreword

A lot of originative ways exist to draw in leads for your business. The key is using promotional strategies that reach the most individuals.

Your attraction strategies will vary depending on what kind of business you own. Net marketers might discover net promotions more advantageous and cost-efficient. Retailers may use programs that get individuals to visit more frequently or make larger purchases.

Whatever the case, your publicities ought to be focused on driving sales and earnings and leads.

Limitless Lead Generation Guide
Turn Yourself Into A Lead Magnet And Vacuum Dry Unlimited Leads To Your Business

Chapter 1:
The Basics

Synopsis

Leads often come in the form of e-mail addresses, behind which are true individuals with very true potential to become your clients, subscribers or members. Having a solid list of leads is assurance that you'll be capable of reaching a ready market and generating revenue from there.

The Beginning

The importance of marketing leads

Companies with a product or service to sell spend billions of dollars on ads alone. That's right – billions. The purpose of spending such a vast amount of cash is mainly to construct buzz about a product, expand the market and finally, bring in better sales.

In small business marketing, the cost of advertising is comparatively small and is paid for by the small business. Your job is to look for a market to promote to that will react to you positively so you may earn an income in return.

This market will come in the form of marketing leads. The quality of these leads, along with the sort and number of positive responses they offer will determine whether or not you'll succeed in marketing. If you hear somebody say, 'the money is on the list', he or she's actually referring to the list of leads. Without this, you can't hope to sell, much less earn.

It's not rocket science, true, but marketing may be tricky nevertheless. It's a proven business model and a lot of people have had considerable success. But, like all businesses, there are also particular factors upon which your success in building your list of marketing leads rest. Consider these factors cautiously:

As a new marketer, you'll find that it will take a while before you may construct your marketing leads. All new marketers have gone through this as enjoying the backing of a solid number of followers won't happen overnight.

To draw in a solid list of marketing leads, you'll have to become a recognized business entity in the industry. Without a reputation, likely leads will find it hard to trust you or at least do business with you. Faced with a choice between purchasing from a popular marketer versus an unfamiliar one, wouldn't you rather purchase from the individual you know than from a total stranger?

The same is true with your marketing leads. They'll need to recognize you as a reliable merchant or affiliate before they agree to purchase, participate or become one of your recruits.

A different key element that affects the number of marketing leads you may obtain is the amount of traffic your site gets. A high web traffic figure is advantageous as it allows you to obtain potentially bigger number of marketing leads.

There are two things that affect how well you may construct your marketing leads. One is the product's value and the other is how well you yourself understand the product.

The choice of a product is critical. A product that has a proven or at least a potential for good sales will be far easier to promote and generate income from. It will too make it easier for you to construct leads with, as leads will be more willing to respond to it.

A great understanding of what makes the product attractive and valuable enough is likewise key to attracting more leads. Being able to explain why and how a product works on your site or articles, for instance, will help you sell it better, particularly vis-à-vis other products competing for the same market.

One common concern among people is market saturation – that point in time when a particular segment of the market becomes inundated with the same (or at least similar) products and services. So much so that it becomes more and more difficult to sell, much less to convince prospective buyers to consider the product or service you're attempting to promote.

You may avoid this, however, by centering on generating affiliate marketing leads from specifically targeted segments of the market or niches. Consider selling or promoting products that appeal to a particular group of individuals who have a common yet largely unmet need. Competition for this market is relatively low and with the right sort of techniques, you'll find that this niche may be especially lucrative.

Chapter 2:
Using News Letters

Synopsis

Newsletters may draw in leads to your business. Individuals tend to purchase from authorities in their field. For example, a business may be more disposed to hire a consultant who authors an e-zine than one that simply advertises online.

If producing e-zines, compile subject matter that helps businesses or consumers with essential issues. For example, as an online designer, you may tell individuals the best place to get complimentary sites.

E-mail people about your gratis newsletter or circulate it in your store. Include data in the newsletter about fresh products or services, along with helpful subject matter.

E-zines

E-zines remain effective communications instrument for businesses, nonprofits, community groups, neighborhoods, special-interest individuals, political activists and other individuals.

E-zines may help hike up sales, raise cash, establish community, organize movements, supply guidance and, naturally, inform a readership. Whether handed over to your letter box or inbox, an e-zine lacking relevant and good articles isn't a great e-zine. If you're utilizing an e-zine, follow the steps below to write effective subject matter.

Comprehend the composition and demographics the e-zine audience and tailor your subject matter accordingly to this constituency's concerns and needs. Think about word count and whether you'll have to supply either photos or graphics to go with the piece.

Study other e-zines to get a feel for the tone (for instance, chatty, formal, academic) and utilize this tone in your subject matter.

Pick out a subject matter topic that you know your subscribers will benefit from or be entertained by.

Compile the subject matter from the third-person perspective to help ensure it's simple for readers to digest.

Put the most crucial, relevant and captivating info at the beginning of the subject matter; less crucial info may be added towards the end. Look to news stories as an example: The information is provided in the descending order of newsworthiness.

Include at least one sidebar, in which key text is visually detached from the main body of the subject matter utilizing a contrasting font or a text-box next to, inside or simply below the subject matter. Popular sidebar material includes lists, resources, facts, how-to directions and quotes.

Proof the subject matter before submitting it.

Chapter 3:
Visualize Goals

Synopsis

How are you utilizing visualization? There are a few likelinesses I may dream up. One, applying a skill or process. Two, the chase of a goal. Three, rivalry, like particular sports and business meetings.

If you're similar to most people, you saw yourself doing it perfectly at once. You succeed big, or you look poised, you acquire a promotion, the hot guys or girls around you faint and fall madly in love. It feels good, strokes your ego, and occasionally step-ups motivation. However for the most part - to put it flat out - it's a waste of time.

See Your Goals

How come? The most crucial consideration is always reality. Mental grooming is an extension of physical grooming. And it's the same with mental conditioning. You have to put yourself in the position as it will be in real life. If it's a work skill, for instance, envisage your surroundings, tools and workmates precisely as they will be. If you're taking on sports, envisage the arena or the court as it will be on the day of the game - down to the weather, the viewers, the clothes you're wearing, and the gear you're using. Make certain to incorporate all your senses, and to make certain you're in the scene - not just thinking about it.

Like every novice, reality has hit me hard if I started sparring ("practice" fighting with an opponent). I got crushed by anybody who had more experience, even the less experienced guys. My strategy fell apart, I had no defense, and I was often paralyzed with fright.

This started to change once I merged realism into my mental grooming. It meant carrying forward my weaknesses and errors. I didn't force that to happen - it came naturally once I made everything as realistic I was able. Even though I was simply sitting on my couch, I felt the canvas under my feet. I smelt the moldy stench of the gym. I felt my shirt holding tight to me, pasty with sweat. I saw the muscles of my sparring mate rippling as his fist came waving at my face. I knew I was getting it correct if my body began stiffening and my heart

started beating rapidly - and if my mental opponent beat me up as he did in the real world.

Did that imply I failed? No, it implied I succeeded. From that point on, I could really begin training. Gradually, I began bettering my defense mentally. My fear diminished. I started picturing the correct attacks and countermoves. These advances, because they came in a realistic scenario, started carrying forward to real life.

Now, a decent add-on is to catch the feelings affected. Have you ever felt it before in the real world? Let's suppose you play basketball. In the real world, you may get the ball through the hoop as frequently as you would like, however there have been times if you have. How did you feel then? Majestic, thrilled?

Try to recall that feeling. Seize it. Expand it if you are able to. Now, hold that feeling while you're rehearsing mentally - it will knock down your learning time. As one Olympic athlete said it, rather than mentally being in the Olympics, he felt it also - he WAS at the Olympics!

Chapter 4:
Blogs

Synopsis

Blogging began as a means of conveying personal thoughts, then it bit by bit became a publicity tool for stars and paparazzi and finally, it reached the entrepreneurs of this globe. With marketing becoming more and more competitive, campaigning through the net ensured that blogging research achieves new peaks.

Writing

Really few models are as popular nowadays as the business blogging model. This is one model where individuals entertain themselves by networking with others, build on their knowledge and, naturally, build on their business leads.

So, aren't you blogging already?

The one matter about blogging that you need to understand is that you are able to monetize it in a lot of different ways. There isn't simply a single way in which you are able to make cash out of a blog; there are many.

Once you have a blog of your own, it is a learning experience in itself. However, at the same time, the cash begins flowing in almost at once, which motivates you into milking your blog further.

Blogging has come a long way from easy web pages to extremely sorted and read material of the net. Comments on blogs and the speed of passing blog links amidst users with similar interest show the use of blogging and its popularity on a global podium.

There are plenty of benefits of blogging for little, big businesses and even the non-trade sections like awareness-creating organizations worldwide. Surveys demonstrate that people prefer to trust those companies more, which lean towards engaging in blogging.

If you get great content on your blog (including keyword optimized text, video recordings and pictures), you are able to be certain that it will get populated soon. The search engines adore blogs because they

get a regular update of content and because so many individuals continue visiting them. In today's scenario, blogs are more effective in sites.

The following are a few ways in which you are able to monetize your blog:-

- You might utilize pay-per-click advertising on your blog.
- You might directly sell or promote products.
- You might give away an eBook or an e-zine subscription and get leads.
- You might build a blog, populate it and then sell the whole thing for a respectable profit.

Chapter 5:
How You See Your Success

Synopsis

Have you settled for what other people have told you success is? There's a science behind every psychological facet that rules our brain. Celebrated philosophers and psychologists have often attempted to explain particular theories and science that rules different parts of our lives. Being comfy within yourself is also one of the sciences that invite happiness.

Every single thought in our brain is like an energy that helps in drawing in events to our life. We act as a magnet that pulls in things from our environment. If you think positive you'll invite favorable outcomes in your life and if you tend to be very negative naturally that will attract negative events in your life. While you need to be positive in life it's likewise crucial that you should be very transparent and not tentative about your thoughts.

Think It

Most individuals admire and respect strong persons, who have won great success by demonstrating will power and self discipline. They look up to individuals, who with sheer self-control, self discipline and ambition, have bettered their life, learned new skills, overcame difficulties and hardships, reduced their weight, climbed high in their chosen field or advanced on the spiritual path.

The reality is that everybody can reach high levels of will power and self-control through a practical method of training. These inner powers are not reserved for a couple of special individuals.

Will power and self-control are two of the most crucial and useful inner powers in everybody's life, and have always been counted as essential tools for success in all areas of life. They can be learned and formulated like any other skill, yet, despite this, only few take any steps to develop and strengthen them in an orderly way.

Willpower is the inner strength to make a decision, take action, and address and execute any aim or task until it's carried out, irrespective of inner and outer resistance, irritation or difficulties.

It contributes the ability to overcome laziness, enticements and negative habits, and to execute actions, even if they call for effort, are unpleasant and tedious or are different than one's habits.

Self discipline is the rejection of instant gratification in favor of something finer. It's the abandoning of instant pleasure and gratification for a higher and finer goal.

It evidences as the ability to stick to actions, views and behavior, which lead to improvement and success. Self-discipline is self-control, and it evidences in spiritual, mental, emotional and physical discipline.

The aim of self-discipline isn't living a confining or a restrictive lifestyle. It doesn't mean being narrow minded. It's among the pillars of success and power. It brings the inner strength to center all your energy on your goal, and persist until it's accomplished.

Both of these abilities are compulsory for daily actions and decisions, and also for making major decisions and arriving at major success. They're required for doing a beneficial job, for studying, building a business, slimming down, bodybuilding and workouts, maintaining good relationships, altering habits, self improvement, meditation, spiritual growth, keeping and accomplishing promises and for almost everything else.

Among the most simple and effective formulas to develop will power and self-discipline is by refusing to fulfill insignificant and unneeded desires. Everybody is constantly confronted and enticed by an endless stream of desires and enticements, many of which are not really crucial or desirable. By learning to deny satisfying every one of them, you get stronger.

Refusing useless, harmful or unneeded desires and actions, and purposely acting contrary to your habits, sharpen and strengthen your inner strength. By ceaseless practice your inner power grows, just like exercising your muscles at a gym increases your physical strength. In both cases, when you require inner power or physical strength, they're available at your disposal.

Here are a few drills:
- Don't read the paper for a day or two.
- Drink water when thirsty, despite your desire to have a soda.
- Walk up and down the stairs, rather than taking the elevator.
- Leave the bus one station before or after your address, and walk the rest of the way.
- Hit the hay one hour earlier than usual.
- If you enjoy ice cream, don't have any for a couple of days.

These are only a couple of illustrations to show how you can develop your will power and self-discipline. You might think that practicing such exercises is being hard on yourself, but they add so much to the storage of your inner strength. By adopting a systematic method of

training you can reach far, have more dominance over yourself and your life, accomplish your goals, and improve your life, and gain satisfaction and serenity.

Show and prove to yourself that you're strong and in control, and rehearse the above exercises for a bit, before passing any judgment on them.

If you prefer to be wealthy work hard but also let your inner self work for you by promoting a thought and idea in your mind that you've already become rich.

Daydream about all those luxuries and services you're going to avail once you're successful. Put down all the positive thoughts you need to cultivate to let your mind work on this positive side. Every idea in your mind works like a thread that gets holds of particular events of your life and controls it to some aspects. Over time you become what you think of and so it's always important that your views are healthy. Nothing is impossible.

Wrapping Up

Stumbling around in the dark looking for leads... no matter what sort of leads... is a pitfall.

Individuals don't just like to hand out their email addresses online (and with great reason today!) However if you offer them something in return, such as an enlightening newsletter, a free eBook, a forum membership or free software, they'll be much more likely to give you their e-mail address when subscribing.

But, do you know why most marketers have a tendency to fail? It's because they bank on their name list a bit much. If I were you, the 1st thing I would do is to get rid of that list of numbers you are currently holding on to.

Here's why - your name list will eventually poop out.

Stop repeating errors!

The definition of insanity is - doing the same thing over and over while expecting different results (this phrase is ironically echoed again and again in net marketing circles!)

There are a lot of ways to render new targeted leads on the Net.

You don't need to meet strangers in a party or collect call cards in supermarkets because it's a very slow and time devouring way to seek targeted leads for your net marketing business.

Studies show that the number 1 issue facing small business owners nowadays is not having enough qualified prospects. Every small business owner would like to have more high-quality candidates, but most either don't have the time, or just don't have the expertise!

In any given industry, there are an infinite number of potential lead sources that can be used to supply your business with highly-qualified sales leads. A few are really simple and inexpensive to set-up, others are more intricate. Some will give you a trickle of leads, others will produce a flood.

The day you stop acquiring fresh leads, your entire business will come to a grating halt - so by establishing a great lead generation system on autopilot, your business will grow by itself, long after you've stopped working on it directly.

www.ingramcontent.com/pod-product-compliance
Lightning Source LLC
Chambersburg PA
CBHW030558220526
45463CB00007B/3111